Leaves

By
Steffi Cavell-Clarke

BookLife PUBLISHING

©2023
BookLife Publishing Ltd.
King's Lynn, Norfolk
PE30 4LS, UK

ISBN: 978-1-80155-918-8

Written by:
Steffi Cavell-Clarke

Edited by:
Charlie Ogden

Designed by:
Danielle Webster-Jones

PHOTO CREDITS

Front cover – alfocome, DPetlia Roman, Nik Merkulov, Kiselev Andrey Valerevich. 1 – italianestro. 2 – Sunny studio. 4 – Romolo Tavani, GongTo. 5 – amenic181, Elena Elisseeva. 6 – Jarous, Ines Behrens–Kunkel. 7 – sevenke, vovan, Carlos Caetano, margaret tong. 8 – Fotofermer, Kazakov Maksim, LubaShi, JOAT. 9 – Miao Liao, Smileus. 10 – Romolo Tavani, rodimov. 11 – alphaspirit, Rock and Wasp, TinnaPong, Alexander Kalina. 12&13 – Dudarev Mikhail. 14 – Thiraphut Anusakulroj , Duct. 15– 88studio, Smit, TungCheung. 16 – Szasz–Fabian Jozsef, Africa Studio. 17 – adike. 18 – Leah–Anne Thompson, Kuttelvaserova Stuchelova. 19 – aleksandr hunta. 20 – Aleksey Stemmer, Ailisa. 21 – melis, Alex Staroseltsev, Kenneth Keifer. 22 – Malivan_Iuliia, Taiga. 23 – Nataliia Melnychuk. All images are courtesy of Shutterstock.com, unless otherwise specified. With thanks to Getty Images, Thinkstock Photo and iStockphoto.

Leaves

CONTENTS

Words that look like **this** can be found in the glossary on page 24.

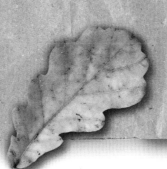

What Is a Plant?

A plant is a living thing. All living things need water, air and **sunlight** to live.

There are many different kinds of plant. Most plants have roots, leaves, flowers and a stem.

Plants live all around the world!

5

What Are Leaves?

Leaves are parts of a plant that grow from the stem and the shoots.

Leaves have a very important job. They make food for the plant!

What Do Leaves Look Like?

Oval

Round

Needle

Long

Leaves come in many different shapes and sizes.

Leaves are usually green, but some change colour at different times of the year.

Many leaves go brown or orange in autumn.

9

How Do Leaves Grow?

As the plant grows, leaves will begin to grow from shoots that branch out from the stem.

The stem of the plant raises the leaves up towards the Sun.

Leaves

Stem

11

Some trees lose their leaves during autumn and winter. The leaves change colour and fall to the ground.

In spring, the trees will grow new leaves.

13

What Do Leaves Do?

The main job of a leaf is to make food for the plant.

14

Leaves **absorb** light from the Sun and gases from the air around them.

15

Leaves need water in order to make food for the plant. They get the water they need from the roots.

The roots absorb water from the ground, which then moves up the stem and into the leaves.

Leaves

The water is carried into the leaves.

Stem

Roots

17

Strange Leaves

The Venus flytrap is a meat-eating plant. When the plant feels an insect on its leaves, it snaps shut!

Stinging nettles have sharp hairs on their leaves. If you touch them, they can make your skin feel very itchy!

19

Leaves on Trees

Deciduous trees

Forests are full of trees that have lots of leaves. Trees that lose their leaves during autumn and winter are called deciduous trees.

Evergreen trees do not lose their leaves during winter. Their leaves are usually thin and spiky.

Evergreen trees

Tasty Leaves

There are lots of leaves that humans can eat. The leaves of lettuces and cabbages are very good for you.

Many animals eat leaves, too. Rabbits, giraffes and koala bears all eat leaves.

23

GLOSSARY

absorb	soak up
forests	areas of land covered in trees
gases	things we cannot see that make up the air around us
grow	naturally develop and increase in size
sunlight	light from the Sun

INDEX